SCHIRMER'S LIBRARY
OF MUSICAL CLASSICS

Vol. 2143

18 ETUDES FOR PIANO

by

Chopin, Debussy, Liszt, Rachmaninoff, Scriabin

CONTENTS

FRÉDÉRIC CHOPIN

2   Etude in E Major, Op. 10, No. 3

6   Etude in C-sharp minor, Op. 10, No. 4

12   Etude in G-flat Major, Op. 10, No. 5

16   Etude in F minor, Op. 10, No. 9

28   Etude in C minor, Op. 10, No. 12

20   Etude in G-flat Major, Op. 25, No. 9

22   Etude in C minor, Op. 25, No. 12

CLAUDE DEBUSSY

33   Pour le cinq doigts d'après Monsieur Czerny from *Etudes*, Livre I

38   Pour les octaves from *Etudes*, Livre I

43   Pour les accords from *Etudes*, Livre II

FRANZ LISZT

48   Transcendental Etude No. 11, "Harmonies du Soir" from *Transcendental Etudes*

60   Etude No. 3, "Un sospiro" from *Three Concert Etudes*

SERGEI RACHMANINOFF

74   Etude-Tableau in C Major from *Etudes-Tableaux*, Op. 33, No. 2

78   Etude-Tableau in G minor from *Etudes-Tableaux*, Op. 33, No. 5

82   Etude-Tableau in A minor from *Etudes-Tableaux*, Op. 39, No. 2

88   Etude-Tableau in E-flat minor from *Etudes-Tableaux*, Op. 39, No. 5

ALEXANDER SCRIABIN

70   Etude in C-sharp minor, Op. 2, No. 1

72   Etude, Op. 65, No. 2

ISBN 978-1-5400-3987-3

G. SCHIRMER, Inc.

DISTRIBUTED BY

HAL•LEONARD®

7777 W. BLUEMOUND RD. P.O. BOX 13819 MILWAUKEE, WI 53213

www.musicsalesclassical.com
www.halleonard.com

à F. Liszt

Etude in E Major

Frédéric Chopin
Op. 10, No. 3

Edited and with fingerings by
Arthur Friedheim

Lento ma non troppo (♪ = 69)

Etude in C-sharp minor

à F. Liszt

Edited and with fingerings by
Arthur Friedheim

Frédéric Chopin
Op. 10, No. 4

à F. Liszt

Etude in G-flat Major

Edited and with fingerings by
Arthur Friedheim

Frédéric Chopin
Op. 10, No. 5

à F. Liszt

Etude in F minor

Edited and with fingerings by
Arthur Friedheim

Frédéric Chopin
Op. 10, No. 9

Edited and with fingerings by
Arthur Friedheim

à Madame la Comtesse d'Agout

Etude in G-flat Major

Frédéric Chopin
Op. 25, No. 9

à Madame la Comtesse d'Agout

Etude in C minor

Frédéric Chopin
Op. 25, No. 12

Edited and with fingerings by
Arthur Friedheim

Allegro molto, con fuoco (♩= 76)

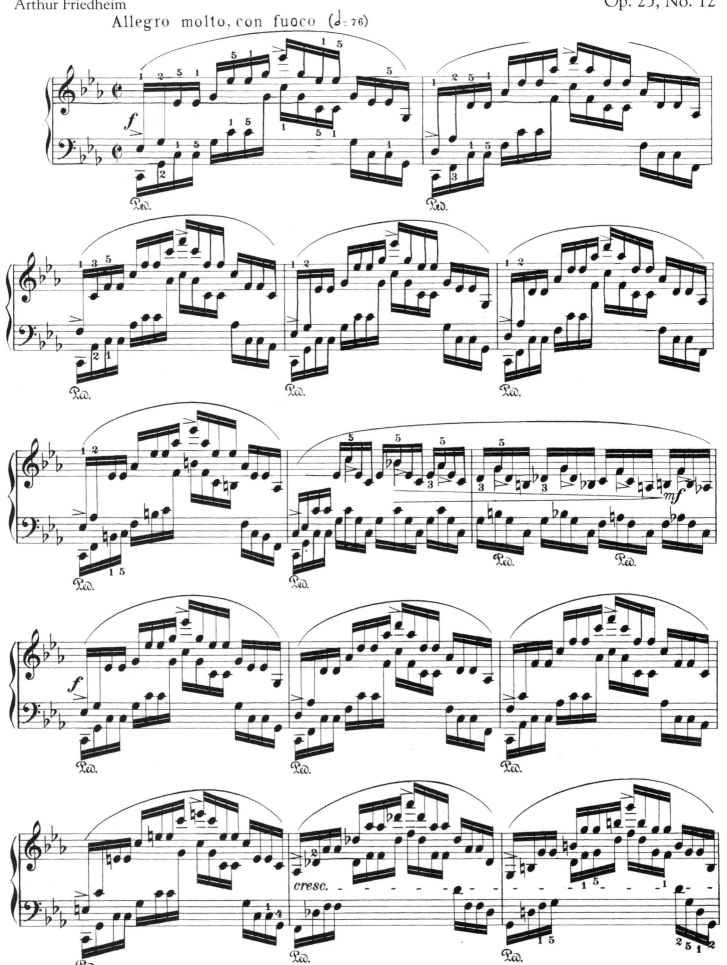

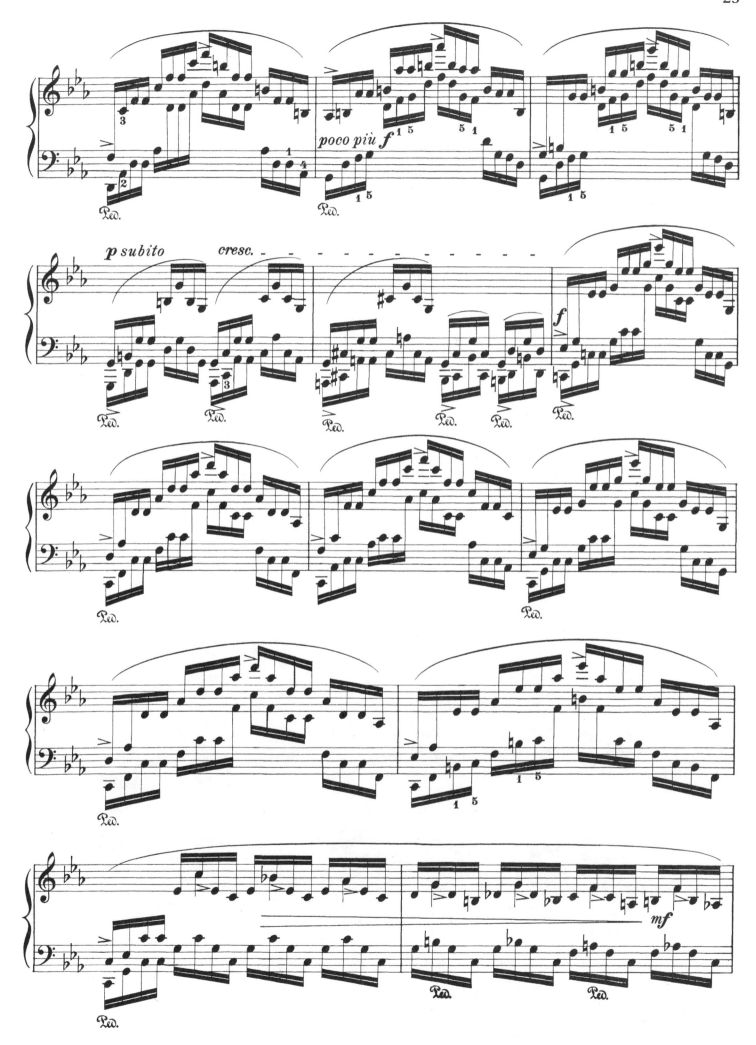

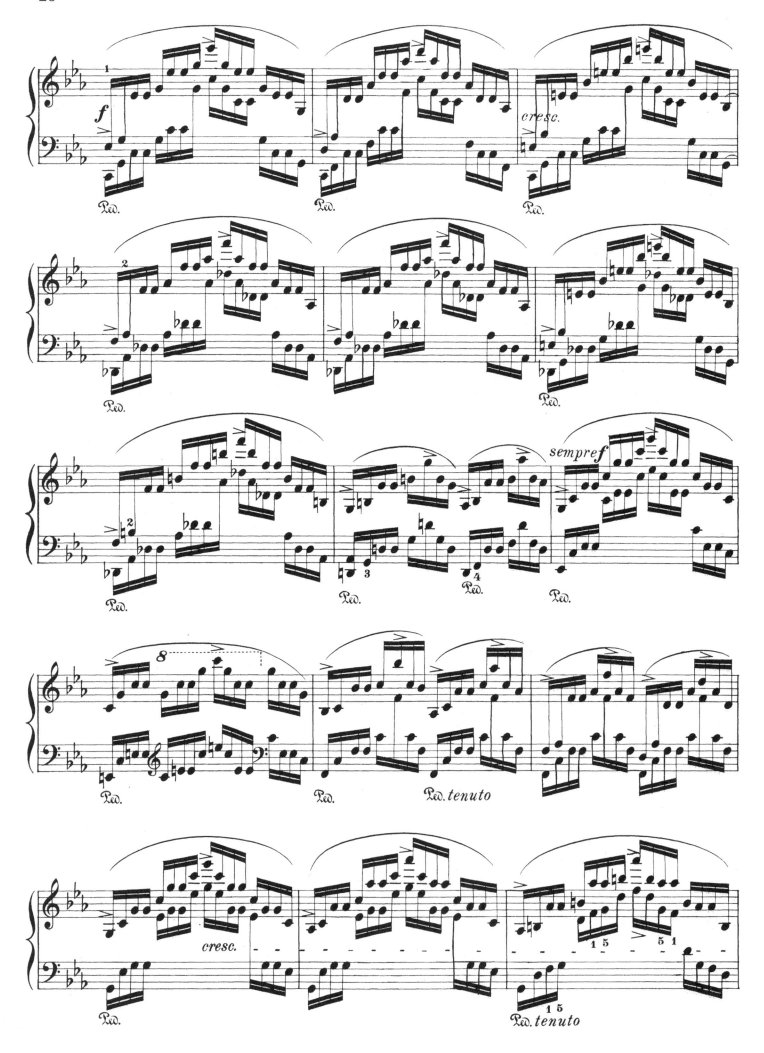

à F. Liszt

Etude in C minor
"Revolutionary"

Edited and with fingerings by
Arthur Friedheim

Frédéric Chopin
Op. 10, No. 12

Allegro con fuoco (♩ = 144)

Pour le cinq doigts d'après Monsieur Czerny

Etude No. 1 from *Etudes*, Livre I

Claude Debussy

Pour les octaves

Etude No. 5 from *Etudes*, Livre I

Claude Debussy

Joyous and carried away, rhythmically free

A Tempo
in ritmo uniforme, senza affrettare

Pour les accords

Etude No. 12 from *Etudes*, Livre II

Claude Debussy

Transcendental Etude No. 11

Harmonies du Soir

from *Transcendental Etudes*

Franz Liszt

Edited and with fingerings by
Paolo Gallico

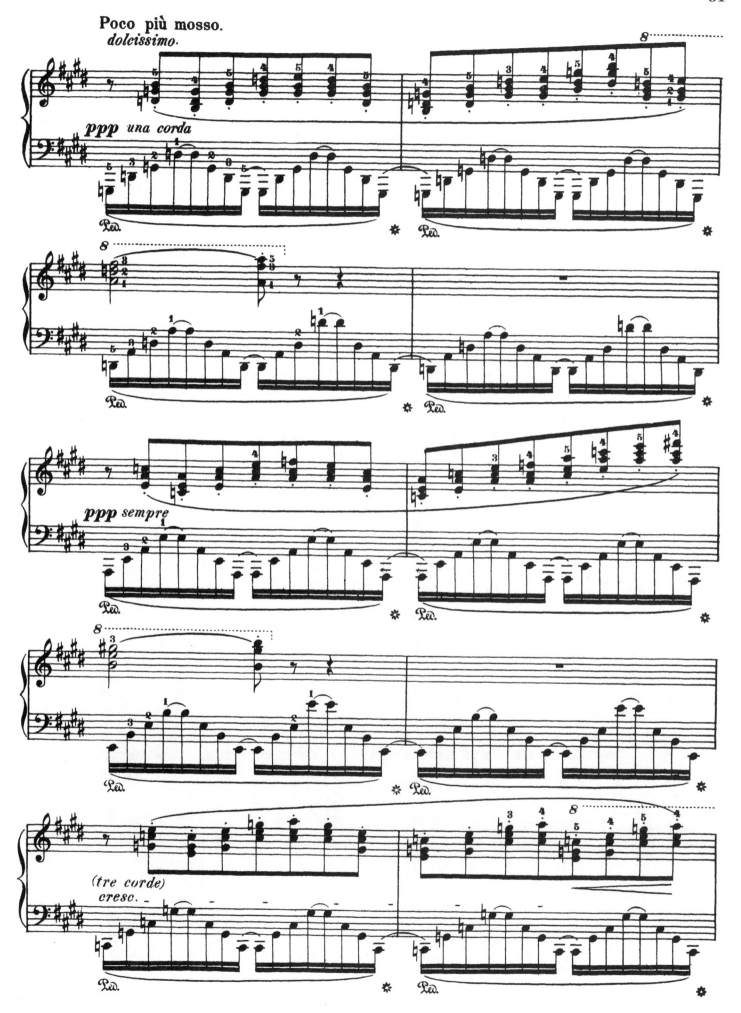

Più lento con intimo sentimento.

accompagnamento quasi Arpa.

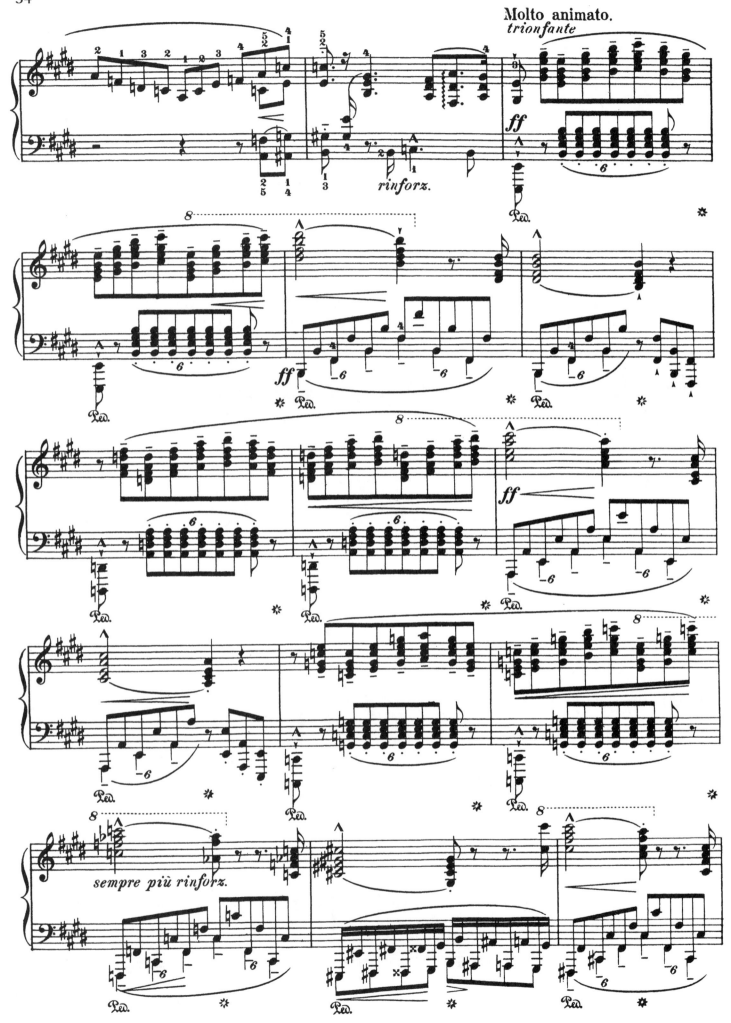

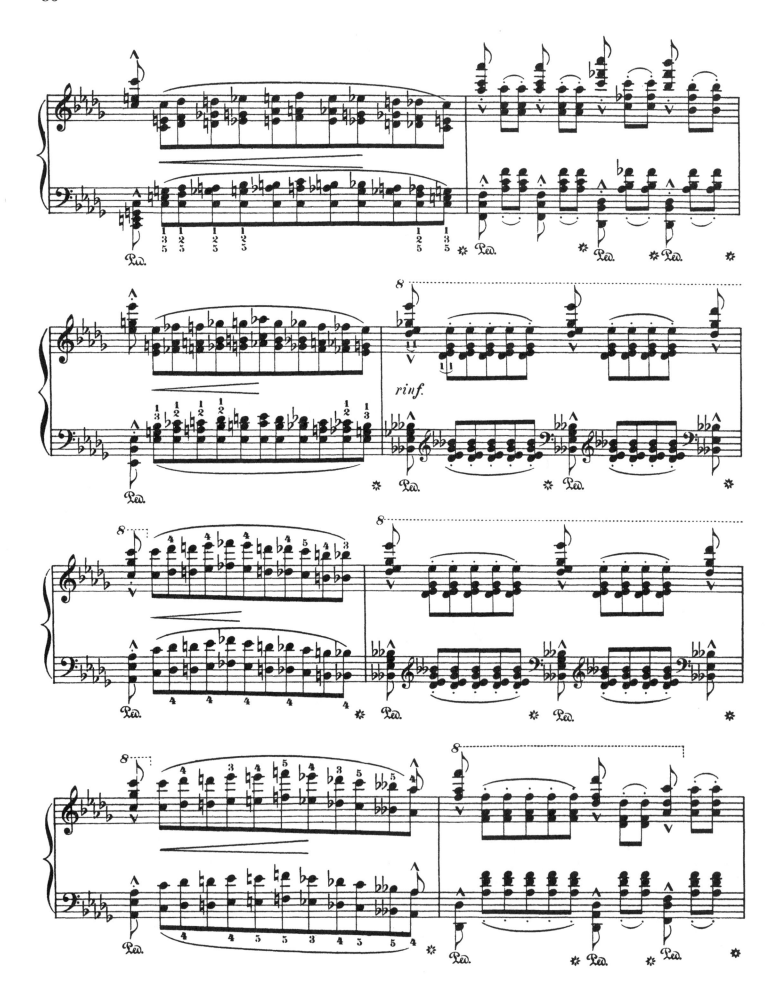

Un sospiro
from *Three Concert Etudes*

Edited and with fingerings by
E. Pauer

Franz Liszt

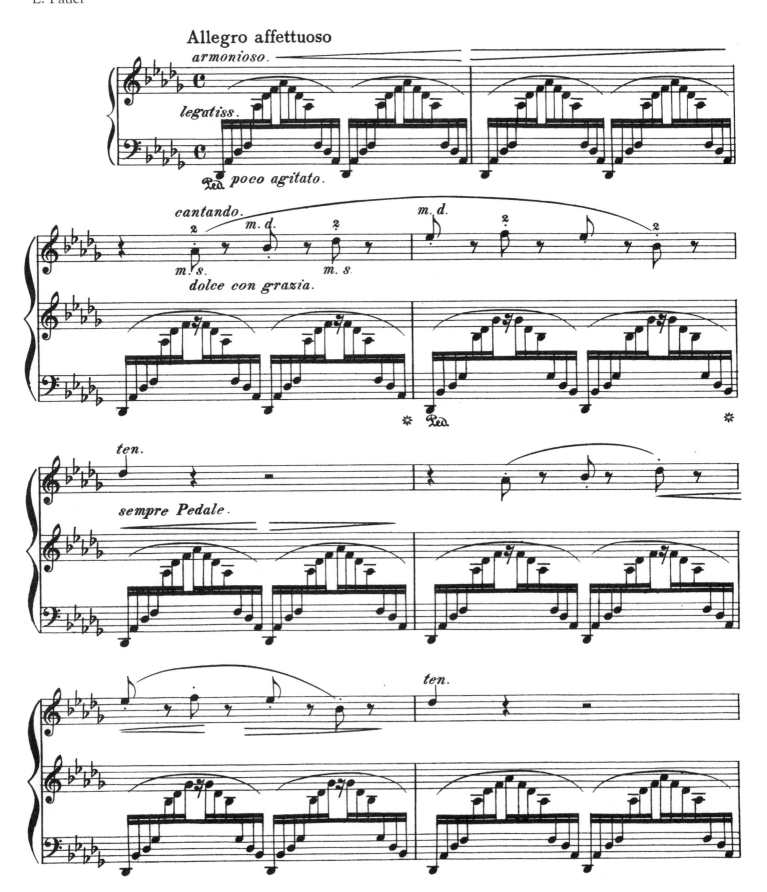

61

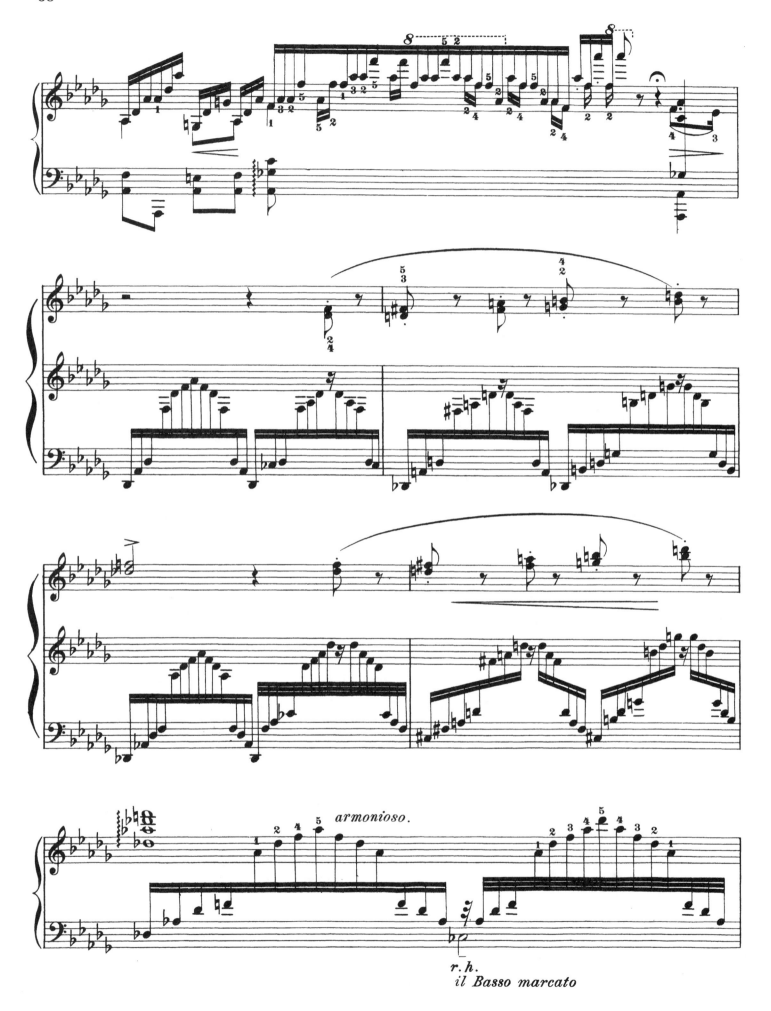

r.h.
il Basso marcato

Etude in C-sharp minor

Alexander Scriabin
Op. 2, No. 1

Edited and with fingerings by
Louis Oesterle

Etude

Alexander Scriabin
Op. 65, No. 2

Etude-Tableau in C Major

from *Etudes-Tableaux*

Sergei Rachmaninoff
Op. 33, No. 2

Etude-Tableau in G minor
from *Etudes-Tableaux*

Sergei Rachmaninoff
Op. 33, No. 5

* Originally, No. 8

Etude-Tableau in A minor

from *Etudes-Tableaux*

Sergei Rachmaninoff
Op. 39, No. 2

Etude-Tableau in E-flat minor

from *Etudes-Tableaux*

Sergei Rachmaninoff
Op. 39, No. 5